Courage Deep Within Me

Ann Winbush

Copyright © 2017 Ann Winbush.

Publisher Name: Visionaries Publishing Press

All rights reserved. No part of this book may be reproduced, stored, or transmitted by any means—whether auditory, graphic, mechanical, or electronic—without written permission of the author, except in the case of brief excerpts used in critical articles and reviews. Unauthorized reproduction of any part of this work is illegal and is punishable by law.

Scripture quotes are taken from the New King James Version®. Copyright © 1982 by Thomas Nelson. Used by permission. All rights reserved.

This book is a work of non-fiction. Unless otherwise noted, the author and the publisher make no explicit guarantees as to the accuracy of the information contained in this book and in some cases, names of people and places have been altered to protect their privacy.

ISBN: 978-0-9989-6550-5 (sc)
ISBN: 978-0-9989-6551-2 (e)

Because of the dynamic nature of the Internet, any web addresses or links contained in this book may have changed since publication and may no longer be valid. The views expressed in this work are solely those of the author and do not necessarily reflect the views of the publisher, and the publisher hereby disclaims any responsibility for them.

Any people depicted in stock imagery provided by Thinkstock are models, and such images are being used for illustrative purposes only. Certain stock imagery © Thinkstock.

Lulu Publishing Services rev. date: 9/1/2017

Contents

Acknowledgement vii
Introduction ix

Do Not Touch 1
The Reveal 2
More than What Meets the Eye 3
Desire for Change 5
Ten Year Span.... Began 6
Mightier 9
The Righteous 10
Understanding 11
Redeemer 12
Family... Secrets Told 13
Twisted Secret 14
Insecurity 15
Answer to Insecurity 16
You Are 18
Mystery Revealed 19
Pressure 20
Feeling Lost 21
Ask a Question? 22
Education 23
THE 24
Out of Darkness into The Light 25
Freedom 26
Unforgiveness 27

Push Back	28
Silenced Know More	29
In need of Love	30
Peace Within	31
Change	32
Joy	33
Brother	34
Appreciative	35
The Word Works	36
Story Told	37
Gentle Touch	38
Insane?	39
Amazing Jesus	40
Aunt	41
I Need You	42
Worship	43
Rain Down	44
Focus	45
Balance?	46
Memory	47
My Daddy	51
What?	53
Time	54
Deep Within	55
Journal	57
Darkness to Light	109
References	129

Acknowledgement

To my wonderful husband, children, family and friends thank you for all your love and support. To the Most High God, Jesus Christ my Lord and Savior and the Holy Spirit teacher of all truth, words cannot express my gratitude toward You for drawing me to You in love. You are my EVERYTHING! I pray as people read this book that You grant them Courage to discover what is "Deep Within" them. I pray clarity and peace in their hearts to rediscover themselves in You... Amen!

Introduction

This book is the result of the God encounters I experienced in a season of my life. The poetry that emerged was locked in a cobwebbed room deep within my heart. I recall, awakening from a deep sleep, as I opened my eyes the words to a poem and title of the poem came out of my mouth. I grabbed a notebook and pen, as the words exude with absolute certainty from my thoughts onto the pages of the notebook. I am astonished, in five minutes I wrote three poems with their titles included. Strangely enough, this happened several times over the course of the next year.

Moreover, I remember giving my testimony in church and I stated that "I was not a poet". I am grateful that the Holy Spirit corrected me by the time I arrived home. From here on, I am whoever God says I am. "A Poet" is one of the many gifts He has placed in me and I accept it.

In the same way, through the inspiration of God the poem entitled "Memory" came into being. In fact, as I drove to church one Sunday morning I could feel a poem emerging from me. All things considered, I was driving and did not have time to pull over. Therefore, I thought to myself record on your phone. Ultimately, I recorded this memory I had of my father when I was about four or five years old on my cell phone as I drove to church. The poem unlocked the door to my past hurt, my current forgiveness and my future healing.

In conclusion, God put it on my heart to include a resource to assist anyone that has experienced challenges with sexual abuse. Be that as it may, the organization I was led to is called Darkness to Light. This organization offers a wealth of knowledge on its website to educate individuals about sexual abuse. Presently, they also offer a training class to help people become facilitators to teach a class on the prevention of sexual abuse.

Above all, as you read the pages to this book I pray that the Holy Spirit will speak to you, reveal to you, and heal you in Jesus name.

Do Not Touch

An unwanted touch on a verge of becoming a woman's body.
Hands that glide and a mind with one objective,
An unwanted touch on a verge of becoming a woman's body.
A shaken and awakening from a man I thought was a Protector,
An unwanted touch on a verge of becoming a woman's body
A voice that speaks with a whisper and a hand to grab
and guide her to a room to receive an unwanted touch
on a verge of becoming a woman's body.
Her mind is racing, body tense, full of anxiety;
An unwanted touch on a verge of becoming a woman's body.
The thoughts are traffic jams running in her head,
how do I escape, I don't want to be in this bed.
This is not right, what is the white stuff?
How long is this going to take, why can't he just leave me alone.
Her heart races and with every unwanted
touch a piece of the little girl dies.
Crying inside acting up outside…
Never happy always scared, ashamed and embarrassed
Don't really know why, just wets the bed…
Why must he take me for the unwanted touch,
I thought he loved me and wanted me untouched.
Why the unwanted touch?
Mommy help me Please!

The Reveal

24 years old life began
I was born again,
Jesus called me in…
To a place of Happiness.
This man Jesus, who I never really knew,
Now drew me in, and I was made brand new.
My heavy heart and low self-esteem drifted away
and myself worth was here to stay.
I could feel the love of God dwelling on the inside
of me, I was developing roots like a tree.
My roots run deep into the sea, for an endless supply of God's
everlasting water that now resides on the inside of me.
His love awakens and reveals the true me.
I was 24 when Jesus came to live on the inside of me.

More than What Meets the Eye

I AM MORE THAN MY OUTER SHELL
I AM MORE THAN WHAT YOU CAN TELL
YOU SEE A SHAPE THAT LOOKS LIKE A
SOUTHERN BELL BUT WAIT
I AM ONLY TWELVE
AS ALL YOU WATCH IS MY TAIL
YOU WAIT AND WAIT IN A SET TRAP FOR AN OPPORTUNITY
TO TOUCH… TO FONDLE… TO ABUSE!
YOU JUST SNAPPED!
I AM MORE THAN MY OUTER SHELL
I AM MORE THAN WHAT YOU CAN TELL
YOU USE MY BODY AS A SEX OBJECT
YOU MOWN AND GROAN…. TOUCH AND FEEL
AS I TRY TO TELL MYSELF JUST STAY STILL.
I STARE OUT THE LITTLE WINDOW OF A
DOOR THAT LEADS TO A SANCTUARY
WHERE WORDS GO FORTH THAT TELL ME
I AM DESERVING
THAT THIS ACTION SHOULD HAPPEN
AFTER MY WEDDING CEREMONY.
MY BODY RESPONSE IN A NEGATIVE WAY;
IT LIKES IT…
IT WANTS IT…
IT DESIRES THE FOUL TOUCH TO STAY.
I AM MORE THAN MY OUTER SHELL AND
MORE THAN WHAT YOU CAN TELL
THE SPIRIT OF LUST WAS PLACED ON ME AT FIVE.

SO, I TOUCHED AND FELT UNTIL I
RECEIVED A TINGLE INSIDE.
WHEN YOU THINK ABOUT IT; THE FACT IT
SHOWED UP IN MY LIFE WAS KNOW SURPRISE.
THE SPIRIT OF PERVERSION WORE ME WELL.
IT USED ME AND ABUSED ME
BUT ... WHO COULD I TELL.
I AM DYING ON THE INSIDE
I AM NOT JUST MY OUTER SHELL
BUT .... WHEN YOU LOOK AT ME YOU CAN'T TELL?
I AM MORE THAN WHAT MEETS THE EYE.

Desire for Change

14 was more than two decades ago
But, I can still remember the desire to let my present life go
I knew something was wrong
That things in my life were not quite right, something
needed to change but I didn't start within
I looked in the mirror and saw an Ugly object and not a friend.
Short skirts, Big earrings and all done Up Hair.
I began to snatch it all off with a feeling that these are not things to wear.
I remember thinking I should look like a Nun
So, I pulled my hair back into a bun.
As I transitioned and God drew me near it was at
this age that I discovered something dear.
A Hunger…
A desire for something more
I didn't know what was in store.
All I knew was I had a Desire for Change…

Ten Year Span.... Began

1981-1991
4 to 14 a ten-year span,
So much has happened where do I began,
I learned to tie my shoe today,
And next year kindergarten is coming my way.
This time is uncertain to me, I just want to be a kid and go outside to play.
From kindergarten to eighth grade,
My sexual appetite is out of control and too much for me to bare.
I have snap shots of images that are to explicit to share.
In this time, period my sins run deep,
Touching private body parts is a part of my life though it shouldn't be.
My mother asked was something going on,
But I was too afraid to answer honestly.
This time span took me for a ride
And killed everything inside me.

1991-2001
14 to 24 a ten-year span,
So much has happened where do I began.
I remember the desire for change to come,
I dropped four boyfriends and only kept one.
I remember at sixteen staying faithful to the one.
I caused so many boys pain,
But in the end that pain came back to me again.
At age 18 I had my precious little girl
By age 20 my wonderful little boy came into the world.
I remember the desire for change coming again at age 23

I met someone that would lead me to a place
where this change could begin…
I visited this church called Straight Gate once or twice
And
At age 24 I was pregnant again
This time with a baby girl and the Holy Spirit was drawing me in.
I remember being nine months pregnant with this baby girl
Walking my hallways feeling different on the inside.
I walked and walked pacing the floor
As tears flowed down,
I said out loud
I WON'T HAVE SEX ANY MORE!
The holy Spirit had come to convict me of my sin;
That day I embarked on a new journey,
Down the path, God had always intended for me.
I had a woman prophesy to me some wonderful things
And gave me instructions from God to develop me.

2001-2011
24 to 34 another ten-year span,
So much has happened where do I began
I join Straight Gate Church, Marry God and take every class I can.
God says that is not enough,
So, I go to college because He says I can.
I tell my mother and grandmother about the sexual abuse
I call one of my abusers and say
I Forgive You
Tears and all I say to myself "I won't let you hurt me again"
I am not dating
Staying faithful to my Heavenly Father
Who is my Man
Six months

Then a Year

God says Wait…. Give me one more year!
Shortly, after this two-year span
I meet a unique young man.
Life moves fast, I look up where am I again
Five years has passed
I am 31 years old, married with four kids… Wait
One more year I own a business, a truck paid for in cash, vacations taken more than twice a year, a 3000-plus sq. ft. home
The blessings of God are flowing in.
Business is great, I get a text from a friend,
God is calling you to a deeper intimacy with Him.
By September 18th of 2011 Blockbuster is having a special
I say to myself my notecards can wait; I deserve a break.
So, from September 18th – October 18th I watched movies and ate.
On October 27th of 2011
God gave me a dream that jerked me straight out of my sleep.
He told me "You are on Assignment!"
So, I began to move my feet.
I got busy in the things of God
Studying my word
Helping my Husband
Praying for people and teaching my children and others about everything God was teaching me.
This experience was so great it changed the atmosphere around me.
2011-2021
34 to 44 I just can't wait to see this ten-year span,
I know so much will happen
So, I will write you at the end.

The Lord on high is mightier
Mightier, than the noise of many waters
Mightier, than the mighty waves of the sea
Your Throne is Established
Your testimonies are Very sure
Holiness forever
Your house O LORD
(Taken from Psalm 93 NKJV)

The Righteous

The righteous shall flourish planted in the house of the LORD
The righteous shall flourish in the courts of our God
Give Thanks to our LORD
O Most High
Your faithfulness loving kindness in the morning
and your faithfulness at night
Still bearing fruit, fresh and flourishing
Your eyes see and your ears hear my desire for righteousness.
(Portions taken from Psalm 92(NKJV)

Understanding

They do not Know nor Understand
They do not consider the Father's Heart and
the Truth that He has Their Hearts
In His hand.
Their Heart is deceived and they have worshiped false gods,
carved images, carnal man or woman that turned away.
A person that is always away in their own
lust, desires, and unbending pride
God,
Deliver their Souls that they might turn back to You and stay.
Stay Away from all things of the flesh
That they may walk as your servant, as your friend
You formed them in their mother's womb.
You are the first and the last.
You who knew know sin became sin.
Please, save them again.
(Portions taken from Isaiah 44 NKJV)

Redeemer

He who formed you from the womb
He who makes all things new
He who stretched out the heavens all alone
He who spread abroad the earth by Himself from His Throne.
He who frustrates the signs of the babblers and drives diviners mad.
He who turns wise men backward,
And makes their knowledge sound sad.
He who confirms the word of His servant and performs
the counsel that He has given to His messengers
He who has Redeemed us from being scavengers…. Amen
(Portions taken from Isaiah 44 NKJV)

Family... Secrets Told

A prayer lifted
To save a dying Soul
A families' secrets finally told
Pray and confess your families' iniquities away.
Freedom in Christ... Freedom that will stay.
Secrets of darkness, pain never told
Finally, Liberty... Freedom in Christ
Our Savior has made us whole.
Light shines in on the darkest of times.
When the flesh is screaming for more time.
It loved to give the unwanted touch generation from generation.
The flesh wanted so much.
The crying of its victims finally told, some healing needed to be whole.
With God's plan now back in place, the legacy
of our family can now be put in place.
Although we cannot erase the past.
God's word will stand and forever last.
We give the enemy no more room.
We will stay in God's word and every family member will be groomed.
We walk in the light of Christ,
We speak the truth,
We make our memories in the light of Christ and this will shine through.
Our family is now in the light, souls saved, flesh
dead, the spirit man quickened and alive.
Finally, Liberty
Freedom in Christ our savior has made us whole.

Twisted Secret

Can you keep a SECRET?
As I take you to a place
Full of Agony, Anguish, and Despair.
Can you keep a SECRET?
As I take you to a place
Pain, Hurt, and Affliction are there.
Can you keep a SECRET?
As I take you to a place
No parents are allowed or loved ones you can trust…
For someone this place is a must.
Can you keep a SECRET?
As I take you to a place
Don't struggle or contest what is going to happen next.
A Life changed forever from a SECRET place of
Torment and Torture
THAT SOMEONE ELSE HOLDS DEAR.

Insecurity

My insecurity lies deep within
It troubles my mind to know end
My insecurity lies deep within
It stirs up fears to know end
My insecurity lies deep within
It brings out doubts to know end
When, How, Where and Why did I develop this insecurity
My soul aches inside.
I pray a change will come
I pray that God's kingdom will come
I pray my needs are met and God's perfect will be done.

Answer to Insecurity

"This hope we have as an anchor of the soul, a hope both sure and steadfast and one which enters within the veil" Hebrews 6:19 (NKJV)
"For I am confident of this very thing, that He who began a good work in you will perfect it until the day of Christ Jesus" Philippians 1:6 (NKJV)
"But seek first the kingdom of God and His righteousness and all these things will be added to you"
Matthew 6:33 (NKJV)
"The LORD is my Shepard I shall not want."
Psalm 23:1(NKJV)
"He will not allow your foot to Slip"
Psalm 121:3 (NKJV)

I Will Not Fear…Hebrew 13:5-6 (NKJV)
Let your conduct be without covetousness
Be content with such things as you have.
For He Himself has said,
"I will never leave you nor forsake you"
So, we may boldly say!
The LORD is my helper; I will not fear.
What can man do to me?
Make sure that your character is free
From the love of money being content with what
you have for He Himself has said,

"I WILL NEVER DESERT YOU, NOR
WILL I EVER FORSAKE YOU"
So, that we confidently say,
The LORD is my helper I will not be afraid.
What will man do to me?

You Are

You are who God said you are
His Beautiful Daughter
His Handsome Son
You are who God said you are
An Overcomer
You are who God said you are
An Answer to someone's prayers
You are who God said you are
So never live in Fear
You are who God said you are
Perfect in His sight
You are who God said you are
So, live for Jesus with all you're might.

Mystery Revealed

Somethings are a Mystery but God is not one
Read His Word!
God is the truth and the life
Read His Word!
He speaks darkness to light
Read His Word!
He tells stories of all His Promises
Read His Word!
He has times, dates, and numbers of the years calculated out for your life.
Read His Word!
Somethings are a Mystery
But God is Not One
Read His Word!

Pressure

I am at home
I am trying to work through
My current Tax situation
Father, I know you have a solution for me.
I asked that you come into my situation.
Help me!
I feel lost and overwhelmed.
So much to do and so little time.
I feel lazy, when I know that I am not,
Could it be my thyroid acting up?
I need a better STRATEGY to get it all done.
I work less at one place.
So, I can build a future for the new place.
Teach Me How to Prosper!
Show Me the Way!
Father God, help me please!
I need You…
I feel like it is too much
I want to work smarter not harder
Eyes are puffy from a lack of sleep
I'm really looking old to me
Help me become that billionaire I see…

Feeling Lost

I feel so lost…
Are you reading God's word?
I feel unmotivated…
Are you reading God's word?
I feel helpless…
Are you reading God's word?
I feel Lost…. Lost…. Lost….
ARE YOU READING GOD'S WORD?

Ask a Question?

Who are you?
What are you wearing?
What are you saying?
Who can see you?
Do you like what you see?
What are you thinking?
Who can you help?
Who can you see?
Where have you been?
Where are you going?
Where are you now?

Education

Education opens doors
Math solves Problems…
I am in a Math Class
I need to Solve Problems
Me and God, Me and Family,
Me and Ministry
Solve Problems
Trying to push and hold on
Wait… God has given me a measure of Faith.
Use my Faith and No Problems can exist.
The Answer is easy
Educate myself in His word…
And live in a Heavenly Bliss.

THE PAIN, THE UNPREDICTABILTIY, THE THOUGHTS, THE SEASON, THE PRAYERS, THE PAIN, THE FAMILY, THE SALON, THE BOUTIQUE, THE CLIENTS, THE STYLIST, THE PAIN, THE GROWTH, THE ACCOMPLISHMENTS, THE STORMS, THE PAIN, THE GROWTH, THE MARRIAGE, THE HUSBAND, THE PAIN, THE SORROW, THE DISAPPOINTMENT, THE GRIEF, THE TIME, THE PATIENCE, THE LOVE, THE CHILDREN, THE JOY, THE COMFORT, THE TIME, THE LESSONS, THE LEARNING, THE LOVE, THE MOTIVATION, THE PASSION, THE WANTS, THE NEEDS, THE HOPE, THE CONFIDENCE, THE PEACE, THE CHURCH, THE TIME, THE NEED, THE PURPOSE, THE HOPE, THE DIFFERENCE, THE MOMENT, THE MINISTRY, THE HAPPINESS, THE SCHOOL, THE STRUGGLE, THE ASSIGNMENT, THE AIM, THE LESSON, THE TEACHER, THE WORK, THE CONCEPT, THE APPLICATION, THE APTITUDE, THE ATTITUDE, THE NEED, THE FIGHT, THE DETERMINATION, THE DRIVE, THE WANT, THE HOLY SPIRIT, THE LOVE, THE JOY, THE PEACE, THE CORRECTION, THE HUNGER, THE THIRST, THE RIGHTEOUSNESS, THE WANT, THE COMFORTER, THE ANSWER, THE KEEPER, THE MASTER, THE SUPPLIER, THE REASON, THE PURPOSE, THE ASSIGNMENT, THE INTERPRETER, THE DELIVER, THE REGULATOR, THE PEACEMAKER, THE PATIENCE, THE GENTLENESS, THE KINDNESS, THE BOLDNESS, THE LOVE, THE REASON, THE BEGINNING, THE END !!!

Out of Darkness into The Light

I can hold you in the darkness of my closet,
Where no light can shine.
The shame and disappointment of the need to want you after
an act or action that is contradictory to my moral beliefs.
I can hold you in the darkness of my closet,
Because I can hide in its darkness and its darkness knows
no shame, embarrassment, nor discomfort.
It is black, pitch black;
No shapes to be seen, and no horror to face.
Eyes cannot see and the brain cannot process logic.
The mind is at rest; ears are soothed with a voice that is familiar,
hands are satisfied to touch a body that is wanted;
In the darkness, I can hold and be held.
In the darkness of my closet
Everything seems to be well...
In the light the truth will prevail.
The reality of the situation is revealed.
Action must take place to find a solution.
The light will not hide anything, nothing
Everything is there to see.
In the light, you must face it,
deal with it, figure it out.
In the light the answers come,
the problems are solved.
The demands are made.
The time is real.
The light is Truth!
The Truth will set you free.

Freedom

Freedom to Love without Shame
Freedom to Hold without Discomfort
Freedom to Trust without Disappointment
Freedom to Dream without Limits
Freedom to Share without Insecurity
Freedom to Hope without Despair
Freedom to Live without Fear
Freedom to Laugh without Crying
Freedom to Be Who God created you to be.

Unforgiveness

Unforgiveness rots out your bones
Brings headaches and stomach stones.
Forgiveness is never about another.
It is God's way to get you to always help and love your sister and brother.
Understanding the root of the problem is sin.
We can't let Satan win.
We know we wrestle not with flesh and blood
Satan influences the mind of the Abuser.
You have every right even, kingdom authority to call out demonic forces.
Don't give up your key to glory.
Bind and Loose… therefore FORGIVE
The power of prayer is within
Use it and never walk in Unforgiveness again.

Push Back when the world pushes in
Push Back and take a God stand
Push Back never give up
Push Back until you win
Push Back through the tears
Push Back even in fear
Push Back using your words
Push Back until you are heard
Push Back with all you're might
Push Back even when they bite
Push Back for what you know is right
Push Back and fight
Push Back using the Word of God
Push Back recite Ephesians 6:10
Push Back walking by faith
Push Back Push Back Push back

Silenced Know More

My voice was silenced as a little girl
The influence of Satan changed my world.
My voice was stolen, killed, and destroyed
I was viewed as a shy, quiet, meek little girl.

My voice was captured and stowed away shipped off to
some foreign land and left me here as silent as a lamb.
My voice was returned to me one Glorious day,
When Jesus Christ called me to Him
And I could say Okay.

In need of Love

In need of love all my life,
Your love God is the only love that will suffice.
You are the ultimate Sacrifice.
Your love found me at my lowest.
In need of love so pure and holy,
God's love will never fail.
My whole being can stand still.
It fills my whole body.
My spirit and soul are satisfied,
Your love surrounds me and brings me peace.
As I battle on until I see…
Victory
Your love continues to lift me.

Peace Within

Peace that calms a stormy rage
Conflictual, conflict within this stage.
Fits of rage and anger screaming within.
Peace come find me,
Search me out,
Help me to survive the calamity that creeped within.
Peace step into my being,
Help me calm a stormy rage,
Help the light out shine the darkness within.
Anxiety, Depression are never my friends
Feed me Peace!
Remind me of how you are and the power you possess.
Help my lips part in Praise,
To our Heavenly Father,
Peace come live within.
Shine bright,
Peace within!

 Change

Be the change you want to see.
Open your eyes,
So, you can clearly be.
Listen good and watch well,
So, you can learn every aspect of the entail.
As you watch the world go around,
You will discover how to change it around.
Be the change you want to see.
It all starts with you,
Helping people be all they can be.
An example, a mentor of sorts is what I mean.
Be the change you want to see.

Joy

What a joy to spend time with You.
To sit and talk with You.
What a joy to have the ear of God
Greatness and Majesty to listen so intensely to little simple me.
What a joy to know I am loved unconditionally.
What a joy to walk and see
Everything my Heavenly Father has made just for me.
What a joy that heaven comes to live all around me.
What a joy that the Creator of all
Has time for me,
To sit and talk,
An ear to hear,
To love and share,
His plan for me.
What a joy God truly loves me.

Brother

Watching a brother is a great thing to see,
I watched my son and my own brothers take care of sisters like me.
They love you,
Protect you and want you to be free.
I watched my husband with his brother and love is all I could see.
He helped him,
Supported him,
And wanted him to be free.
I watched my brother get married,
And raise a family.
Love is what I could see.
He sacrificed for the three.
Watching a brother is a great thing to see.
The love and dedication each one can or could bring.
An inspiration in God's creation.... Brother

Appreciative

Casting my cares on You, it leaves me nothing
else to do but to focus in on You.
Teaching people through You
Loving people through You
Learning people through You
Helping people through You
Meeting people through You
Working through You
Casting my cares on You, it leaves me nothing
else to do but to focus in on You.
I am Appreciative.

The Word Works

Listen young people the word of God works,
It works in you to help develop you.
It fills you to teach you.
It stretches you to new levels.
Listen young people the word of God works,
It comes to build your faith,
To cause action in your heart and mind to move
you closer to the plan of God for your life.
Listen young people the word of God works.
It answers every concern.
Solution to every situation.
It is always there to support,
Encourage,
And to put love in you,
The Word Works…

Story Told

What role do you play in another's Story Told?
Are you a Helper?
Are you a Teacher?
Are you a Mentor?
Are you a Motivator?
What do you bring to another person's Story Told?
Is it Positive?
Is it Exciting?
Is it Energizing?
Is it Encouraging?
What do you bring to your own Story Told?
Is it Fun?
Is it Bright?
Is it full of Life?
Is it full of Love?
Whatever we do,
Whatever we say,
Let it be full of God's story already told.

Gentle Touch

Oh, how I long for a gentle touch,
How I lay in bed feeling alone.
When there is someone by me,
But seems to be in a distant place…
How much longer can I stay in this race.
How I long for a gentle touch
I am married
But still lack so much.
Jesus help me please…
How do I cope with this tease?
He touched me for his satisfaction alone.
It leaves me feeling all alone.
How can we fix this please?
God, I am on my knees,
I pray for this cycle to end.
Father, please help my husband touch me again.

Insane?

If I'm insane… it is for you LORD!
If I'm crazy… it is for you LORD!
If I'm loony… it is for you LORD!
If I'm nuts…. It is for you LORD!
If I'm cuckoo… it is for you LORD!
If I'm certifiable…. It is for you LORD!
If I'm hysterical… It is for you LORD!
If I'm bananas… it is for you LORD!
If I'm off my rocker… it is for you LORD!
If I've ever lost my mind
It is so I could find it in you…LORD!
My heart beats for you.
My soul thirst for you.
My spirit is connected to you.
I hunger for you.

Amazing Jesus

Amazing, Amazing
Jesus
Amazing, Amazing, Amazing
Jesus
Amazing
Jesus
So, Amazing to me.
Amazing Jesus
The one who died and rose again
Took the keys from hell that I may bind and loose the captives free.
Amazing, Amazing
Jesus
Sits at the right hand of the Father making intercession for me.
Amazing, Amazing, Amazing,
Jesus!

Aunt

As I reflect on a face that looks so close to mine.
As the tears roll down,
I search for words,
I cannot Find.
She meant so much to me,
She was so dear…
I miss her
I miss her
I miss her being so near…
A phone call or a car ride away.
She would call me Bert
And I would answer
Okay.
She would say Darling, with so much excitement it filled the air,
And every time after I finished doing her hair….
"More Hair"
she would speak into the atmosphere.
She made sure I would see her.
She tried her best to prepare me.
I thought my prayers were working.
But she didn't want to stay.
She said I would be Okay,
But it doesn't feel that way.
I loved her
She loved me
She was my Aunt
And I am her Niece.

 I Need You

Lord, I need You.
Cast my cares on You.
You supply all my needs.
All things are possible with You.
Please show me your plan and how to execute,
To live in it!
To eat of its fruit…
Please let me rest in Your love for me.
Your love for me
Your love for me
Your love for me
Your love for me
Your love for me

Worship

I worship You my King,
King of Kings
Lord of Lords
Almighty God.
I worship You my King,
King of Kings
Lord of Lords
Almighty God.
I worship You,
I worship You,
With all my heart
With all my soul
With all my strength
With all my mind
I worship You.

Rain Down

Rain Down
You heavens from above and let the skies pour down righteousness;
Rain Down
Let the earth open,
Let them bring forth salvation.
Mercy and Truth
Righteousness and Peace
Yield Increase
Rain Down
Let righteous spring up
The Lord has created it
Righteousness makes his footsteps our path.
Rain down
Rain down
Yield Increase.
(Taken from Isaiah 45 NKJV)

Focus

Focus on the Joy of Life
Not the Pain
Focus on the Joy of Life
Because that will Sustain
Focus on the Joy of Life
Not the Pain
Focus on the Joy of Life
That will bring you Gain
Focus on the Joy of Life
Not the Pain
Focus on the Joy of Life
It will lift the Stain
Focus on the Joy of Life
Jesus is that Joy
Focus
Focus
Focus
Jesus!

Balance?

Does Balance Even Exist?
I know people don't give you Balance
They will keep you in Suspense
Balance
That comes from Above
Just learn to walk in Love
Learning to prioritize is the best you can Do
Don't worry about hurting peoples feeling; let God lead You
People don't give you Balance
You set the Tone
People don't give you Balance
They murmur and Complain
Because you manage your Time
They want to steal and abuse
For them time is all the Same
No need to Balance
No need to Prioritize
No Plans
No place to Be
Just living life Openly
I believe a prioritized life is as balanced as you Get
Does Balance Even Exist?

I have this picture that I can see,
I can see it, clearly of this man that I truly love so dearly.
I remember walking around on a couch.
As I watched him pinch this rolled up piece of paper in-between his fingers so strangely, and move it to his mouth.
This man that I love so dearly, I remember walking back and forth hugging him on the couch.
Thinking to myself…I love him so much, so clearly, he means the world to me.
This man inspires me, I call this man my daddy.
Never could I have seen what the future would hold for me.
When this man would come, and get me later in the night to do things I knew wasn't right.
Father God, I don't know You yet.
But I know You know me.
So, help me through this mess.
He has a need that he needs filled.
He just doesn't realize… I'm not the thrill.
He's killing me slowly on the inside each time.
I don't understand Lord help me stop crying.
I don't want to go.
I just want to stay in my bed.
Father God, please keep me safe.
I don't want Ted!
Ted is a man that Satan has influenced.

He does not realize that his mind has been captured, that
Satan has entered through a gate, a portal that he opened
when he spoke words of hatred and uncertain.
He spoke words that he would never be abused, but he
would become the abuser and choose. So, he chose to
abuse without even knowing this is what he did.
And hurt someone so deeply,
These scars are heal-able the memories will fade.
They will never completely go away, but God's word sustains.
Father, I Thank You for every experience I've had.
Without You in my life it would be…
So, Sad!
I wouldn't walk, I couldn't talk, my voice was silenced, because of it.
But because of You, I speak again so clearly, and loud.
You resonate on the inside of me, more than I can explain.
Your love is so great it overshadows each pain.
Lord, You pour your spirit into me like no other.
Every bad decision I made it doesn't matter,
not to me nor to others.
You use my testimony as inspiration to inspire;
them to come out of their mess.
To desire… You Lord
To desire … more Lord to have the life that You had planned for them.
Father, it's all possible!
Father, I Thank You so much.
You mean so much to me.
Father, I couldn't say it enough.
As I speak tears roll down my eyes to know the victims that still cry inside.
They have no one to share their pain with, no one to hug Lord.
They don't understand that they are not alone.
That they are not the first to go down this ugly road.
But You God,

But You God,
You never have left us.
You are always there with us, and I Thank You for that.
You Lord,
You Lord, are the reason why we breathe.
You are the reason why we survive Lord, and I Thank You for that.
My heart pours out in an abundance of laughter, because I understand and know Lord that You are my Captain.
You are the Bishop of my soul,
You carry me through.
Every storm Lord,
Every obstacle, You see me through.
I Thank You Father God for who You are to me, because of You I can be free.
I love You so much and I will not ever live in despair because I know You rule and You reign and You will always be there.
You are here,
There,
You are everywhere.
You touch me Lord.
You heal me Lord.
You created me to be something greater than I could ever see.
Because of my testimony some that are broken will be restored.
They will no longer suffer in discord.
I Thank You that I understand that we wrestle not against flesh and blood.
That You bring us to repentance.
Conviction Lord God, You bring so we can be restored.
You draw us closer to You, as only You can do.
I Thank You so much, You are the hero that I seek.
You're the one I want to be like… Lord because You made me.
You called me from my mother's womb.
You helped me see something greater in me…

Lord,
I Thank You so much for loving me, for never leaving me even in my mess,
You knew I would confess.
Thank You! Jesus Christ for calling me home that I can dwell in You,
My Shepherd,
My King, that sits on the throne.
I Thank You for that.

My Daddy

I could see God's glory… it sat on a man I call daddy.
We've had some rough spots in our past, but thank God, we are free at last.
One thing I can truly say is that I could see
God's glory sit on my daddy today.
God has changed him, it's so plain to see, my daddy cares for me.
If he could take it all back, change what he did
the hurt, the pain. The sadness he did…
He would.
Oh, if he could
But we can start right here rebuild, and restore
My daddy loves me
My daddy loves me
I didn't choose him God decided he would be
the man that was to protect me.
He did what he knew how.
His life was full of self- hatred and doubt.
How could he give me something he didn't have?
The love of God was not in his eyes.
He chased a different path of sin years ago
Thank God for the power of prayer
Somebody had to pray that somebody is me.
I prayed so hard for God to save me and my daddy
I prayed the same prayer for him as I did for me
Breakthrough came.
Now our lives have changed.
Forgiveness
Came in the atmosphere it changed everything that I held so dear.
I could see the Glory of God Today!

As I looked in my daddy's eyes on this God given glorious day.
He spoke words to encourage me, to lift me up higher
You see My daddy truly loves me.
I know, I know he hurt me years ago, but God
knew I would heal and move in His flow;
The flow of the Holy Spirit that heals that
comes to quicken my mortal body…
I can't sit still.
I must share this awesome testimony.
What God has done in our Family.
He took what Satan meant for evil and turned it for our good.
My job is just beginning, I must go far and wide
to tell the story of Bertha and Ted.
My daddy loves me!
My daddy loves me instead.
God can use all our mess we must understand
it's only a test to see our Faith rise
To see our story told
To see another life, unfold.
To change another family that is in despair.
My dad and I will team up to stop the madness to stop
the crook that comes to steal, kill, and destroy.
But Jesus
But Jesus
Who can compare. He came that we would have life abundantly.
Yes, I saw the Glory of God sit on my daddy…
Who cares what you did in the past.
Let by gone be by gone
And just move along.…….
God loves you and me.
Forgive yourself for not loving you.
How can you love someone else if you can't first love you?
I saw the Glory of God sit on my daddy today.

What?

What can you do when you hate you?
When you look in the mirror and it's still you.
This ugly face looking back at you.
What can you do?
When your skin crawls at the sight of you,
When your stomach turns at the thought of you.
What can you do to replace the feelings inside
of self-hatred and low-self-esteem?
First face the demon in the mirror you see
Tell that Devil it must Flee.
Recite what God says about you
I am made in God's image and likeness
I am a child of God
I am a friend of Jesus
I am important
I am loved
I am beautiful
I am justified and redeemed through Christ
I am not condemned by God
I am accepted by Christ Jesus
I am valuable
My body is the temple of the Holy Spirit
I am a new creature in Christ
I am as God sees me
I am His beloved
I am a creator and I speak these things that God
says about me into existence in my life. |

 Time

It's time to pursue
It's time to execute
The gifts will make room for you
Go into the world and spread the gospel
Teach God's word to all that you see
Share God's word with a lot of company
It's time to pursue
It's time to execute
The gifts will make room for you
Go into the world and see the beautiful people God has created to be
His children
His servants
His friends
They do exist.
Teach God's word with a large amount of company
Teach and Share
Teach and Share
Pursue and Execute
Pursue and Execute
It is Time.

Deep Within

Deep within me
Deep within me
Deep within me you will go
My story
Your story told
I will go
Deep within me
My story
My story
Deep within me your story glows
I will go deep within me,
Oh, Oh, Oh my soul.
I will go
You are my King
You are my King, that sits on the throne.
Deep within me my story, your story told
Deep within me your story glows.

Take a moment to reflect,
Revisit pages 21, 22, 46, and 53 and answer
the set of questions that you see.
I pray this will awaken the poet that you can
be. Then continue to journal away,
Exploring your thoughts each day.

Habakkuk 2: 2-3 (NKJV) Then the LORD answered me and said: "Write the vision and make it plain on tablets, that he may run who read it. For the vision is yet for an appointed time; But at the end it will speak, and it will not lie. Though it tarries, wait for it; Because it will surely come, It will not tarry"

CONTACT

VisionariesHairStudio.com
Visionariesboutique.com
Poshmark@visionaries
Amazon.com/visionaries
Twitter: @_visionaries
Instagram: visionaries boutique
YouTube: Ann Winbush Step By Step
Facebook: visionaries boutique
Facebook: Ann Winbush

DARKNESS TO LIGHT

CHILD SEXUAL ABUSE STATISTICS

The Issue of Child Sexual Abuse

What is child sexual abuse?

FACT: The definition of child sexual abuse is broader than most people realize.

Often a traumatic experience for children and teens, child sexual abuse is a criminal offense punishable by law in many societies.[1]

Child sexual abuse includes:

- any sexual act between an adult and a minor, or between two minors, when one exerts power over the other.[1]
- forcing, coercing or persuading a child to engage in any type of sexual act.[1]
- non-contact acts such as exhibitionism, exposure to pornography, voyeurism, and communicating in a sexual manner by phone or Internet.[1]

What is the magnitude of the problem?

FACT: Child sexual abuse is far more prevalent than most people realize.

- Child sexual abuse is likely the most prevalent health problem children face with the most serious array of consequences.[2]
- About one in 10 children will be sexually abused before their 18th birthday*.[1]
- About one in seven girls and one in 25 boys will be sexually abused before they turn 18*.[1]
- This year, there will be about 400,000* babies born in the U.S. that will become victims of child sexual abuse unless we do something to stop it.[1]

*Includes contact abuse only

FACT: Identified incidents of child sexual abuse are declining, although there is no clear indication of a cause.

- The number of identified incidents of child sexual abuse decreased at least 47% from 1993 to 2005-2006.[3,4]

FACT: Even with declining rates of sexual abuse, the public is not fully aware of the magnitude of the problem.

- The primary reason is that only about 38% of child victims disclose the fact that they have been sexually abused.[5,6] Some never disclose.[7,8]
- There are also privacy issues surrounding cases of child sexual abuse. For instance, public police reports do not name the victim, and most media concerns have a policy that precludes naming victims.

FACT: Most people think of adult rape as a crime of great proportion and significance, and are unaware that children are victimized at a much higher rate than adults.

- Nearly 70% of all reported sexual assaults (including assaults on adults) occur to children ages 17 and under.[9,10] Youths have higher

rates of sexual assault victimization than do adults. In 2000, the rate for youths aged 12 to 17 was 2.3 times higher than for adults. [53]
- 44% of rapes with penetration occur to children under age 18. Victims younger than 12 accounted for 15% of those raped, and another 29% of rape victims were between 12 and 17. [10,11]

Who are the perpetrators of child sexual abuse?

FACT: Those who molest children look and act just like everyone else. There are people who have or will sexually abuse children in churches, schools and youth sports leagues.

Abusers can be neighbors, friends and family members. People who sexually abuse children can be found in families, schools, churches, recreation centers, youth sports leagues, and any other place children gather.

Significantly, abusers can be and often are other children.

- About 90% of children who are victims of sexual abuse know their abuser.[12,13] Only 10% of sexually abused children are abused by a stranger.[12]
- Approximately 30% of children who are sexually abused are abused by family members.[12,13]
- The younger the victim, the more likely it is that the abuser is a family member. Of those molesting a child under six, 50% were family members. Family members also accounted for 23% of those abusing children ages 12 to 17.[9]
- About 60% of children who are sexually abused are abused by people the family trusts.[12,13]
- Homosexual individuals are no more likely to sexually abuse children than heterosexual individuals.[15]

FACT: Not everyone who sexually abuses children is a pedophile.

Child sexual abuse is perpetrated by a wide range of individuals with diverse motivations. It is impossible to identify specific characteristics that are common to all those who molest children.

- Situational offenders tend to offend at times of stress and begin offending later than pedophilic offenders.
- They also have fewer victims (often family), and have a general preference for adult partners.[16]
- Pedophilic offenders often start offending at an early age, and often have a large number of victims (frequently not family members).[16]
- 70% of child sex offenders have between one and 9 victims, while 20% have 10 to 40 victims.[14]

FACT: As many as 40% of children who are sexually abused are abused by older, or more powerful children.[12]

- The younger the child victim, the more likely it is that the perpetrator is a juvenile. Juveniles are the offenders in 43% of assaults on children under age six. Of these offenders, 14% are under age 12.[9]
- Juveniles who commit sex offenses against other children are more likely than adult sex offenders to offend in groups, to offend at schools, and to have more male victims and younger victims.[11]
- The number of youth coming to the attention of police for sex offenses increases sharply at age 12 and plateaus after age 14. Early adolescence is the peak age for youth offenses against younger children.[14]
- A small number of juvenile offenders — one out of eight — are younger than age 12. Females constitute 7% of juveniles who commit sex offenses.[14]

FACT: Most adolescent sex offenders are not sexual predators and will not go on to become adult offenders.

- Most adolescent offenders do not meet the criteria for pedophilia and do not continue to exhibit sexually predatory behaviors.[39]
- Adolescent sex offenders are more responsive to treatment than adults. They do not appear to continue to reoffend into adulthood, especially when provided with appropriate treatment.[29]

Risk Factors and Consequences

Under what circumstances does child sexual abuse occur?

FACT: Child sexual abuse often takes place under specific, often surprising circumstances.

It is helpful to know these circumstances because it allows for the development of strategies to avoid child sexual abuse.

- 81% of child sexual abuse incidents for all ages occur in one-perpetrator/one-child circumstances. Six to 11year-old children are most likely (23%) to be abused in multiple-victim circumstances.[9]
- Most sexual abuse of children occurs in a residence, typically that of the victim or perpetrator – 84% for children under age 12, and 71% for children aged 12 to 17.[9]
- Sexual assaults on children are most likely to occur at 8 a.m., 12 p.m. and between 3 and 4 p.m. For older children, aged 12 to 17, there is also a peak in assaults in the late evening hours.[9]
- One in seven incidents of sexual assault perpetrated by juveniles occurs on school days in the after-school hours between 3 and 7 p.m., with a peak from 3 to 4 pm.[9]

FACT: Commercial sexual exploitation and internet sex crimes against children are a small and yet significant part of the overall problem.

- In 2006, arrests for online youth victim cases constituted only 1.2% of arrests for all sex crimes against children. There were 615 arrests for online cases vs. 49,345 arrests for all sex crimes against children.[18]
- 9% of all 10 to 17 year olds receive unwanted sexual requests while on the Internet.[19]
- Over a period of one year, one in 25 youth received an online sexual solicitation where the solicitor tried to make offline contact.[20]
- 23% of all 10 to 17 year olds experience unwanted exposure to pornography.[19]
- Child sexual abuse makes children more vulnerable to sexual exploitation. More than 90% of children who are commercially sexually exploited have been sexually abused in the past.[21]
- About 75% of child pornography victims are living at home when they are photographed. Parents are often responsible.[21]

FACT: Abusers often form relationships with potential victims and their families prior to the abuse. This is called "grooming."

Grooming is a process by which an offender gradually draws a victim into a sexual relationship and maintains that relationship in secrecy. At the same time, the offender may also fill roles within the victim's family that make the offender trusted and valued.

Grooming behaviors can include:

- Special attention, outings, and gifts
- Isolating the child from others
- Filling the child's unmet needs
- Filling needs and roles within the family

- Treating the child as if he or she is older
- Gradually crossing physical boundaries, and becoming increasingly intimate/sexual Use of secrecy, blame, and threats to maintain control

What factors increase a child's risk for sexual abuse?

FACT: While no child is immune, there are child and family characteristics that significantly heighten or lower risk of sexual abuse.

The following risk factors are based on reported and identified cases of abuse:

- Family structure is the most important risk factor in child sexual abuse. Children who live with two married biological parents are at low risk for abuse. The risk increases when children live with stepparents or a single parent.[3]
- Children living without either parent (foster children) are 10 times more likely to be sexually abused than children that live with both biological parents. Children who live with a single parent that has a live-in partner are at the highest risk: they are 20 times more likely to be victims of child sexual abuse than children living with both biological parents.[3]
- Gender is also a major factor in sexual abuse. Females are five times more likely to be abused than males.[30] The age of the male being abused also plays a part. 8% of victims aged 12 to 17 are male. 26% of victims under the age of 12 are male.[9]
- Age is a significant factor in sexual abuse. While there is risk for children of all ages, children are most vulnerable to abuse between the ages of seven and 13.[30] The median age for reported abuse is nine years old.[31] However, more than 20% of children are sexually abused before the age of eight.[9]

- Race and ethnicity are an important factor in identified sexual abuse. African American children have almost twice the risk of sexual abuse than white children. Children of Hispanic ethnicity have a slightly greater risk than non-Hispanic white children.[3]
- The risk for sexual abuse is tripled for children whose parent(s) are not in the labor force.[3]
- Children in low socioeconomic status households are three times as likely to be identified as a victim of child abuse.[3]
- Children who live in rural areas are almost two times more likely to be identified as victims of child sexual abuse.[3]
- Children who witness or are the victim of other crimes are significantly more likely to be sexually abused.[32]

FACT: Family and acquaintance child sexual abuse perpetrators have reported that they look for specific characteristics in the children they choose to abuse.

- Perpetrators report that they look for passive, quiet, troubled, lonely children from single parent or broken homes.[17]
- Perpetrators frequently seek out children who are particularly trusting Find new and work proactively to establish a trusting relationship before abusing them.[51] Not infrequently, this extends to establishing a trusting relationship with the victim's family as well.[17]

What are the immediate consequences of child sexual abuse?

FACT: Emotional and mental health problems are often the first consequence and sign of child sexual abuse.

- Children who are sexually abused are at significantly greater risk for later posttraumatic stress and other anxiety symptoms depression and suicide attempts. [7, 23, 24, 35, 36, 37, 38, 39, 40, 41, 42, 49, 50, 51, 52, 53]

- These psychological problems can lead to significant disruptions in normal development and often have a lasting impact, leading to dysfunction and distress well into adulthood.[35, 42,43,44,45]
- Behavioral problems, including physical aggression, non-compliance, and oppositionality occur frequently among sexually abused children and adolescents.[7,54,111,112]
- Child sexual abuse has been linked to higher levels of risk behaviors.[22,47,4]

FACT: Sexual behavior problems and over-sexualized behavior are a very common consequence of child sexual abuse.

Age-inappropriate behavior can be a very important and telling sign that abuse is occurring.

Children who have been sexually abused have over three times as many sexual behavior problems as children who have not been sexually abused.[46]

- Victims of child sexual abuse are more likely to be sexually promiscuous.[54,55,56]

FACT: Academic problems in childhood are a common symptom of sexual abuse.

- Sexually abused children tended to perform lower on psychometric tests measuring cognitive ability, academic achievement, and memory assessments when compared to same-age non-sexually abused cohorts.[60]
- Studies indicate that sexual abuse exposure among children and adolescents is associated with high school absentee rates, more grade retention1, increased need for special education services and difficulty with school adaptation.[61]

- 39% of 7 to 12-year-old girls with a history of child sexual abuse had academic difficulties.[62]
- 7 to 12 year-old girls with a history of child sexual abuse were 50% more likely to display cognitive ability below the 25th percentile.[62]
- 26% of 7 to 12 year-old girls with a history of child sexual abuse reported that their grades dropped after they were abused and 48% had below-average grades.[62]
- A history of child sexual abuse significantly increases the chance of dropping out of school.[35,61,62,63]

FACT: Substance abuse problems beginning in childhood or adolescence are some of the most common consequences of child sexual abuse.

- A number of studies have found that adolescents with a history of child sexual abuse demonstrate a three to fourfold increase in rates of substance abuse/dependence.[22,23,47,48,64]
- Drug abuse is more common than alcohol abuse for adolescent child sexual abuse victims. Age of onset for non-experimental drug use was 14.4 years old for victims, compared to 15.1 years old for non-victimized youth.[65]
- Adolescents were 2 to 3 times more likely to have an alcohol use/dependence problem than nonvictims.[65]

FACT: Delinquency and crime, often stemming from substance abuse, are more prevalent in adolescents with a history of child sexual abuse.

- Adolescents who were sexually abused have a 3 to 5-fold risk of delinquency.[23,37,66,67,68,69]
- Behavioral problems, including physical aggression, non-compliance, and oppositionality occur frequently among sexually abused children and adolescents.[70]

- These emotional and behavioral difficulties can lead to delinquency, poor school performance and dropping out of school.[35,61,62,63]
- Adolescents that reported victimization (i.e., sexual abuse or physical abuse) were more likely to be arrested than their non-abused peers.[66,67]
- Sexually abused children were nearly twice as likely to run away from home.[66]

FACT: The risk of teen pregnancy is much higher for girls with a history of child sexual abuse. The increased risk for pregnancy at a young age is likely due to over-sexualized behavior, another common consequence of child sexual abuse.

- Girls who are sexually abused are 2.2 times as likely as non-abused peers to become teen mothers.[40,54]
- 45% of pregnant teens report a history of child sexual abuse.[40]
- Males who are sexually abused are more likely than their non-abused peers to impregnate a teen. In fact, several studies indicate that the sexual abuse of boys is a stronger risk factor for teen pregnancy than the sexual abuse of girls.[59,72,83]

Most sexual abuse incidents reported by pregnant teens occurred well before the incident that resulted in pregnancy. Only 11 to 13% of pregnant girls with a history of child sexual abuse reported that they had become pregnant as a direct result of this abuse.[72]

What are the long-term consequences of child sexual abuse?

Child sexual abuse has lasting consequences for victims. The real tragedy is that it robs children of their potential, setting into motion a chain of events and decisions that affect them throughout their lives.

FACT: Substance abuse problems are a common consequence for adult survivors of child sexual abuse.

- Female adult survivors of child sexual abuse are nearly three times more likely to report substance use problems (40.5% versus 14% in general population).[74]
- Male adult CSA victims are 2.6 times more likely to report substance use problems (65% versus 25% in general population).[74]

FACT: Mental health problems are a common long-term consequence of child sexual abuse.

- Adult women who were sexually abused as a child are more than twice as likely to suffer from depression as women who were not sexually abused.[75]
- Adults with a history of child sexual abuse are more than twice as likely to report a suicide attempt.[76,77]
- Females who are sexually abused are three times more likely to develop psychiatric disorders than females who are not sexually abused.[78,79,80]
- Among male survivors, more than 70% seek psychological treatment for issues such as substance abuse, suicidal thoughts and attempted suicide.[81]

FACT: Obesity and eating disorders are more common in women who have a history of child sexual abuse.

- 24 year-old women who were sexually abused as children were four times more likely than their nonabused peers to be diagnosed with an eating disorder.[82]
- Middle-aged women who were sexually abused as children were twice as likely to be obese when compared with their non-abused peers.[75]

FACT: Child sexual abuse is also associated with physical health problems in adulthood. It is theorized that this is a consequence of the substance abuse, mental health issues and other consequences that survivors of child sexual abuse face.

- Generally, adult victims of child sexual abuse have higher rates of health care utilization and report significantly more health complaints compared to adults without a child sexual abuse history.[83,84,85] This is true for both self-reported doctor's visits and objective examination of medical records.[86] These health problems represent a burden both to the survivor and the healthcare system.
- Adult survivors of child sexual abuse are at greater risk of a wide range of conditions that are non-life threatening and are potentially psychosomatic in nature. These include fibromyalgia, severe premenstrual syndrome, chronic headaches, irritable bowel syndrome and a wide range of reproductive and sexual health complaints, including excessive bleeding, amenorrhea, pain during intercourse and menstrual irregularity.[49,87,88,89]
- Not only do survivors of child sexual abuse have more minor health conditions, they are at greater risk for more serious conditions as well. Adults with a history of child sexual abuse are 30% more likely

than their non-abused peers to have a serious medical condition such as diabetes, cancer, heart problems, stroke or hypertension.[84]

Male sexual abuse survivors have twice the HIV-infection rate of non-abused males. In a study of HIVinfected 12 to 20 year olds, 41% reported a sexual abuse history.[90, 91]

FACT: Adult survivors of child sexual abuse are more likely to become involved in crime, both as a perpetrator and as a victim. This is likely a product of a higher risk for substance abuse problems and associated lifestyle factors.

- Adult survivors are more than twice as likely to be arrested for a property offense than their non-abused peers (9.3% versus 4.4%).[66]
- As adults, child sexual abuse victims were almost twice as likely to be arrested for a violent offense as the general population (20.4% versus 10.7%).[66]
- Males who have been sexually abused are more likely to violently victimize others.[81]

Note: Although survivors of child sexual abuse are negatively impacted as a whole, it is important to realize that many individual survivors do not suffer these consequences. Child sexual abuse does not necessarily sentence a victim to an impaired life.

Child sexual abuse has lasting consequences for societies. When the prevalence of child sexual abuse is combined with its economic burden, the results are staggering.

FACT: Child sexual abuse is a public health problem of enormous consequence.

- The CDC recently estimated the lifetime burden of a new substantiated of nonfatal child maltreatment to be $210,012 per victim. This includes immediate costs, as well as loss of productivity and increased healthcare costs in adulthood.[92]
- While this estimate is for all forms of child maltreatment, there is evidence that the consequences of child sexual abuse are equivalent or greater than the consequences of other forms of child maltreatment.[4]
- This estimate is comparable to that of many other high profile public health problems, indicating the impact and seriousness of the issue of child maltreatment. For example, the lifetime costs of stroke per person were estimated at $159,846 (2010 dollars).The total lifetime costs associated with type 2 diabetes were estimated between $181,000 and $253,000 (2010 dollars) per case.[92]

Reporting Child Sexual Abuse

What are the reporting rates for child sexual abuse?

FACT: Only about a third of child sexual abuse incidents/cases are identified, and even fewer are reported.

Researchers estimate that 38% of child victims disclose the fact that they have been sexually abused.[5,6] Of these, 40% tell a close friend, rather than an adult or authority.[7] These "friend-to-friend" disclosures do not always result in reports. This means that the vast majority of child sexual abuse incidents are never reported to authorities, though research suggests that disclosure rates to authorities may be increasing.[24]

- Child protective services agencies investigate about 55% of the child sexual abuse incidents reported to them. The rest are "screened out" for lack of adequate information or for other reasons. Of those reports investigated, only a portion meets the criteria for "substantiated."3
- Child protective service agencies investigate only 20% of the incidents/children identified and reported by school personnel.3

School personnel identify 52% of all identified child abuse cases classified as causing harm to the child, more than any other profession or organizational type, including child protective services agencies and the police.3

- Two-thirds of teachers do not receive specific training in preventing, recognizing or responding to child sexual abuse in either their college coursework or as part of their professional development.[25]
- 24% of school personnel have never received any oral or written guidelines on the mandated reporting requirements of their state.[3]
- As many as 25% of child sexual abuse incidents identified by professionals not working specifically in child protection services are not reported, despite a mandated reporting law that requires it.[3]

FACT: False reports of child sexual abuse made by children are rare.

It is estimated that only 4 to 8% of child sexual abuse reports are fabricated. Most of the fabricated reports are made by adults involved in custody disputes or by adolescents.[26]

How many child sexual abuse reports result in arrests?

FACT: A large number of those arrested for child sexual assault are convicted and serve time in prison or jail.

While the rate of conviction is high, arrests are made in only 29% of child sexual abuse cases and are 32% more likely to be made in incidents involving older children. For children under six, only 19% of sexual abuse incidents result in arrest.[9]

- Of those charged, about 80% of rape offenders (including rapists of adults) are convicted.[27]
- An estimated 48% of rape defendants (including rapes of adults) were released from detention prior to the disposition of their case. Only defendants charged with murder had a lower rate of release (24%) than those for whom rape charges were ending.[11]
- About 14% of those convicted of rape were convicted in a jury trial, but for most defendants (82%), conviction followed a guilty plea. The remaining 4% were convicted following a bench trial.[11]
- Overall, 87% of convicted rapists (including rapists of adults) were incarcerated, and about 13% received a sentence to probation supervision in the community.[11]
- For convicted rapists sentenced to prison (not local jails), the average term imposed was just under 14 years. An estimated 2% of convicted rapists received a term of life imprisonment.[11]
- For each convicted rape offender in a prison or jail, there are nearly 3 rape offenders under probation or parole supervision in the community.[11]

Fact: Research shows that child sexual abuse perpetrators re-offend at a lower rate than other types of offenders, including those convicted of rape.

- Rapists had a lower rate of re-arrest for a new felony and a lower rate of re-arrest for a violent felony than most categories of probationers with convictions for violence.[11,28]
- Released rapists were found to be 10.5 times as likely as non-rapists to be re-arrested for rape.[11]
- Research suggests that incest offenders re-offend at approximately half the rate of "acquaintance" child molesters.[28]

What do I do if I suspect or discover child sexual abuse?

FACT: Signs that a child is being sexually abused are often present, but they are often indistinguishable from other signs of childhood stress, distress or trauma.

- Direct physical signs of child sexual abuse are not common. However, when physical signs are present, they may include bruising, bleeding, redness and bumps, or scabs around the mouth, genitals, or anus. Urinary tract infections, sexually transmitted diseases, and abnormal vaginal or penile discharge are also warning signs.[33,34]
- Child sexual abuse victims often exhibit indirect physical signs, such as anxiety,[33,34] chronic stomach pain and headaches.[35,36,37,38,39,40,41]
- Emotional and behavioral signals are common among sexually abused children. Some of these are "too perfect" behavior, withdrawal, fear, depression, unexplained anger and rebellion.[33,34,35, 42,43,44,45]
- Some common consequences of trauma include nightmares, bedwetting, falling grades, cruelty to animals, bullying, being bullied, fire setting, runaway, and self-harm of any kind.[33,34]

- One of the most telling signs that sexual abuse is occurring is sexual behavior and language that is not age-appropriate.[33,34,46]
- Use of alcohol or drugs at an early age can be a sign of trauma such as child sexual abuse.[22,23,33,34,47,48]

Note: Child sexual abuse victims may exhibit a wide range of immediate reactions, both in magnitude and form. Resilient children may not suffer serious consequences, whereas other children with the same experience may be highly traumatized. Some victims do not display emotional problems or any other immediate symptom in response to the abuse.

FACT: Child sexual abuse reports should be made to the state's child protective services agency, the police or both. Visit www.D2L.org/gethelp for more information.

Facts taken from Darkness to Light, Used by
Permission, All Rights Reserved

Darkness to Light
7 Radcliffe Street, Suite 200
Charleston, SC 29403
D2L.org
1-843-965-5444

REFERENCES

1. Townsend, C., & Rheingold, A.A., (2013). Estimating a child sexual abuse prevalence rate for practitioners: studies. Charlesto Darkness to Light. Retrieved from www.D2L.org.

   Townsend, C. (2013). Prevalence and consequences of child sexual abuse compared with other childhood experiences.

2. Charleston, S.C., Darkness to Light. Retrieved from www.D2L.org.

   Sedlak, A.J., Mettenburg, J., Basena, M., Petta, I., McPherson, K., Greene, A., and Li, S. (2010). Fourth National Incidence

3. Study of Child Abuse and Neglect (NIS–4): Report to Congress, Executive Summary. Washington, DC: U.S. Department of Health and Human Services, Administration for Children and Families.
4. Finkelhor, D., & Jones, L. (2012). Have sexual abuse and physical abuse declined since the 1990s? Durham, NH: Crimes against Children Research Center. http://www.unh.edu/ccrc/pdf/CV267_Have%20SA%20%20PA%20Decline_FACT%20SHEET_11-7-12.pdf
5. London, K., Bruck, M., Ceci, S., & Shuman, D. (2003) Disclosure of child sexual abuse: What does the research tell us about the ways that children tell? *Psychology, Public Policy, and Law, 11*(1), 194-226.
6. Ullman, S. E. (2007). Relationship to perpetrator, disclosure, social reactions, and PTSD symptoms in child sexual abuse survivors. *Journal of Child Sexual Abuse, 16*(1), 19-36.
7. Broman-Fulks, J. J., Ruggiero, K. J., Hanson, R. F., Smith, D. W., Resnick, H. S., Kilpatrick, D. G., & Saunders, B. E. (2007). Sexual

assault disclosure in relation to adolescent mental health: Results from the National Survey of Adolescents. *Journal of Clinical Child and Adolescent Psychology*, 36, 260 – 266.
8. Smith, D. W., Letourneau, E. J., Saunders, B. E., Kilpatrick, D. G., Resnick, H. S., & Best, C. L. (2000). Delay in disclosure of childhood rape: Results from a national survey. *Child Abuse & Neglect*, 24, 273 – 287.
9. Snyder, H. N. (2000). Sexual assault of young children as reported to law enforcement: Victim, incident, and offender characteristics. Washington, DC: U.S. Department of Justice, Office of Justice Programs, Bureau of Justice Statistics. Retrieved January 12, 2009 from*http://www.ojp.usdoj.gov/bjs/pub/pdf/saycrle.pdf*
10. National Crime Victimization Survey, Statistic calculated by staff at Crimes against Children Research Center. 2002.
11. Greenfeld, L.A. (1997). Sex Offenses and Offenders An Analysis of Data on Rape and Sexual Assault. U.S. Department of Justice, Office of Justice Programs, Bureau of Justice Statistics, NCJ-163392
12. Finkelhor, D. (2012). Characteristics of crimes against juveniles. Durham, NH: Crimes against Children Research Center.
13. Whealin, J. (2007-05-22). "Child Sexual Abuse". National Center for Post Traumatic Stress Disorder, US Department of Veterans Affairs.
14. Finkelhor, D., Ormrod, R., Chaffin, M. (2009) Juveniles who commit sex offenses against minors. Juvenile Justice Bulletin, OJJDP, Office of Justice Programs
15. Jenny, Carole, Roesler, Thomas A., Poyer, Kimberly L. (1994) Are children at risk for sexual abuse by homosexuals? Pediatrics, Vol. 94 No. 1, pp. 41-44.
16. Abel, G. G., Mittleman, M. S., & Becker, J. V. (1985). "Sex offenders: Results of assessment and recommendations for treatment." In M. H. Ben-Aron, S. J. Hucker, & C. D. Webster (Eds.), Clinical Criminology: The assessment and treatment of criminal behavior (pp. 207–220).
17. Elliott, M., Browne, K., & Kilcoyne, J. (1995). Child sexual abuse prevention: What offenders tell us. Child Abuse & Neglect, 5, 579-594.

18. Wolak, J., Finkelhor, D., Mitchell, K. (2006). Trends in arrests of online predators. Department of Justice, Office of Juvenile Justice and Delinquency Prevention Report. Crimes Against Children Research Center, University of New Hampshire.
19. Jones, L,. Mitchell, K., Finkelhor, D. (2012). Trends in youth internet victimization: Findings from three youth internet safety surveys 2000–2010, Journal of Adolescent Health 50: 179–186.
20. Wolak, J., Finkelhor, D., Mitchell, K., Ybarra, M. (2008) "Online "Predators" and their Victims: Myths, Realities and Implications for Prevention and Treatment" published by American Psychologist, 63(2), 111-128
21. National Institute of Justice. (2007). Commercial sexual exploitation of children: What do we know and what do we do about it? (Publication NCJ 215733). US Department of Justice. Office of Justice Programs.
22. Walker, E.A. Gelfand, A., Katon, W.J., Koss, M.P, Con Korff, M., Bernstien, D., et al. (1999). Medical and psychiatric symptoms in women with children and sexual abuse. Psychosomatic Medicine, 54, 658-664.
23. Kilpatrick, D. G., Ruggiero, K. J., Acierno, R., Saunders, B. E., Resnick, H. S., & Best, C. L. (2003). Violence and risk of PTSD, major depression, substance abuse/dependence, and comorbidity: Results from the National Survey of Adolescents. Journal of Consulting and Clinical Psychology, 71, 692-700.
24. Finkelhor, D., Ormrod, R., Turner, H. A., & Hamby, S. L. (2012). Child and youth victimization known to school, police, and medical officials in a national sample of children and youth. Juvenile Justice Bulletin, (No. NCJ 235394). Washington, DC: United States Department of Justice, Office of Juvenile Justice and Delinquency Prevention.
25. Kenny, M.C. (2004). Teachers' attitudes toward and knowledge of child maltreatment. Child Abuse and Neglect, 28, 1311-1319.
26. Everson, M., and Boat, B. (1989). False allegations of sexual abuse by children and adolescents.Journal of the American Academy of Child and Adolescent Psychiatry. 28, 2:230-35.

27. Walsh, W.A., Jones, L., Cross, T.P., Lippert, T. (2008). Prosecuting child sexual abuse: The importance of evidence type. Crime Delinquency OnlineFirst, doi:10.1177/0011128708320484
28. Grossman, L., Martis, B., Fichtner, C. (1999). Are sex offenders treatable? A research overview.Psychiatric Services 50 (3): 349–361
29. Association for the Treatment of Sexual Abusers (ATSA). (2000). The effective legal management of juvenile sex offender. Retrieved from www.atsa.com/ppjuvenile.html
30. Finkelhor, D. (1994). Current information on the scope and nature of child sexual abuse. The Future of Children, Vol. 4, No. 2, Sexual Abuse of Children, pp. 31-53
31. Putnam, F. (2003). Ten-year research update review: Child sexual abuse. Journal of the American Academy of Child and Adolescent Psychiatry, 42, 269-278.
32. Finkelhor, D., Ormrod, R.K. & Turner, H.A. (2010). Poly-victimization in a national sample of children & youth. American Journal of Preventive Medicine.
33. Prevent Child Abuse America (2003). Recognizing child abuse: What parents should know. Chicago, IL. Retrieved 5-31-2013 from www.preventchildabuse.org.
34. Stop It Now! (2013) Warning signs in children and adolescents of possible child sexual abuse.Northampton, MA. Retrieved 5-31-2013 from www.stopitnow.org
35. Saunders, B.E., Kilpatrick, D.G., Hanson, R.F., Resnick, H.S., & Walker, M. E. (1999). Prevalence, case characteristics, and long-term psychological correlates of child rape among women: A national survey. Child Maltreatment, 4, 187-200.
36. Grayson, J. (2006). Maltreatment and its effects on early brain development. Virginia Child Protection Newsletter, 77, 1-16.
37. Leeb, R., Lewis, T., & Zolotor, A. J. (2011). A review of physical and mental health consequences of child abuse and neglect and implications for practice. American Journal of Lifestyle Medicine, 5(5), 454-468.

38. Friedrich, W.N., Fisher, J. L., Dittner, C.A., Acton, R, Berliner, L, Butler, J., Damon, L., Davies, W.H., Gray, A. & Wright, J. (2001). Child Sexual Behavior Inventory: Normative, psychiatric, and sexual abuse comparisons. Child Maltreatment, 6, 37-49.
39. McLeer, S. V., Dixon, J. F., Henry, D., Ruggiero, K., Escovitz, K., Niedda, T., & Scholle, R. (1998). Psychopathology in non-clinically referred sexually abused children. Journal of the American Academy of Child and Adolescent Psychiatry, 37, 1326 – 1333.
40. Noll, J. G., Shenk, C. E., & Putnam, K. T. (2009). Childhood sexual abuse and adolescent pregnancy: A meta-analytic update. Journal of Pediatric Psychology, 34, 366-378.
41. Olafson, E. (2011). Child sexual abuse: Demography, impact, and interventions. Journal of Child & Adolescent Trauma, 4(1), 8-21.
42. Banyard, V. L., Williams, L. M., & Siegel, J. A. (2001). The long-term mental health consequences of child sexual abuse: An exploratory study of the impact of multiple traumas in a sample of women. Journal of Traumatic Stress, 14, 697 – 715.
43. Molnar, B. E., Buka, S. L., & Kessler, R. C. (2001). Child sexual abuse and subsequent psychopathology: Results from the National Comorbidity Survey. American Journal of Public Health, 91, 753 – 760.
44. Polusny, M. A., & Follette, V. M. (1995). Long-term correlates of child sexual abuse: theory and review of the empirical literature. Applied and Preventive Psychology, 4, 143 – 166.
45. Young, M. S., Harford, K., Kinder, B., & Savell, J. K. (2007). The relationship between childhood sexual abuse and adult mental health among undergraduates: Victim gender doesn't matter. Journal of Interpersonal Violence, 22, 1315 – 1331.
46. Girardet, R. G., Lahoti, S., Howard, L. A., Fajman, N. N., Sawyer, M. K., Driebe, E. M., et al. (2009). Epidemiology of sexually transmitted infections in suspected child victims of sexual assault. Pediatrics, 124, 79-84.

47. Acierno, R., Kilpatrick, D. G., Resnick, H. S., Saunders, B., de Arellano, M. & Best, C. (2000). Assault, PTSD, family substance use, and depression as risk factors for cigarette use in youth: Findings from the national survey of adolescents. Journal of Traumatic Stress, 13, 381-396.
48. Felitti, V.J., Anda, R.F., Nordenberg, D., Williamson, D., Spitz, A.M., Edwards, V., Koss, M., Marks, J.S., (1998) Relationship of childhood abuse and household dysfunction to many of the leading causes of death in adults: The adverse childhood experiences (ACE) study. American Journal of Preventive Medicine 14(4).
49. Lanier, P., Jonson-Reid, M., Stahlschmidt, M. J., Drake, B., & Constantino, J. (2010). Child maltreatment and pediatric health outcomes: A longitudinal study of low-income children. Journal of Pediatric Psychology, 35(5), 511-522.
50. Mullers, E. S., & Dowling, M. (2008). Mental health consequences of child sexual abuse. British Journal of Nursing, 17(22), 1428-1433.
51. De Bellis, M. D., Spratt, E. G., & Hooper, S. R. (2011). Neurodevelopmental biology associated with childhood sexual abuse. Journal of Child Sexual Abuse, 20(5), 548-587.
52. Cohen, E., Groves, B., & Kracke, K. (2009). Understanding children's exposure to violence. The Safe Start Center Series on Children Exposed to Violence, 1, 1-8.
53. Tebbutt, J., Swanston, H., Oates, R. K., O'Toole, B.I. (1997). Five years after child sexual abuse: Persisting dysfunction and problems of prediction. Journal of the American Academy of Child & Adolescent Psychiatry, 36, 330-339.
54. Noll, J.G., Trickett, P.K., & Putnam, F.W. (2003). A prospective investigation of the impact of childhood sexual abuse on the development of sexuality. Journal of Consulting and Clinical Psychology, 71, 575-586.
55. Paolucci, E.O, Genuis, M.L, & Violato, C. (2001). A meta-analysis of the published research on the effects of child sexual abuse. Journal of Psychology, 135, 17-36.

56. Kellogg, N.D., Hoffman, T.J, & Taylor, E.R. (1999). Early sexual experience among pregnant and parenting adolescents. Adolescence, 43, 293-303.
57. Moran, P. B., Vuchinich, S., & Hall, N. K. (2004). Associations between types of maltreatment and substance use during adolescence. Child Abuse and Neglect, 28(5), 565–574. doi:10.1016/j.chiabu.2003.12.002
58. Finkelhor, D., & Ormrod, R. K. (1999). Reporting crimes against juveniles. Juvenile Justice Bulletin, (No. NCJ 178887). Washington, DC: United States Department of Justice, Office of Juvenile Justice and Delinquency Prevention.
59. Saewyc, E.M., Magee, L.L., & Pettingall, S.E. (2004). Teenage pregnancy and associated risk behavior among sexually abused adolescents. Perspectives on Sexual and Reproductive Health, 36(3), 98-105.
60. Wells, R., McCann, J., Adams, J., Voris, J., & Dahl, B. (1997). A validational study of the structured interview of symptoms associated with sexual abuse using three samples of sexually abused, allegedly abused, and nonabused boys. Child Abuse & Neglect, 21, 1159-1167.
61. Reyome, N.D. (1994). Teacher ratings of the academic achievement related classroom behaviors of maltreated and non-maltreated children. Psychology in the Schools, 31, 253-260
62. Daignault, I.V. & Hebert, M. (2009). Profiles of school adaptation: Social, behavioral, and academic functioning in sexually abused girls. Child Abuse & Neglect, 33, 102-115.
63. Rice, D. P., & Miller, L. S. (1996). The economic burden of schizophrenia: Conceptual and methodological issues, and cost estimates. In M. Moscarelli, A. Rupp, & N. Sartorious (Eds.), Handbook of mental health economics and health policy. Vol. 1: Schizophrenia (pp. 321–324). New York: John Wiley and Sons.
64. Briere, J., & Elliott, D.M. (2003). Prevalence and psychological sequelae of self-reported childhood physical and sexual abuse in a general population sample of men and women. Child Abuse & Neglect, 27(10), 1205-1222.

65. Harrison, P. A., & Narayan, G. (2003). Differences in behavior, psychological factors, and environmental factors associated with participation in school sports and other activities in adolescence. Journal of School Health, 73(3), 113–120. doi:10.1111/j.1946-1561.2003.tb03585
66. Siegal, J.A. & Williams, L.M. (2003). The relationship between child sexual abuse and female delinquency and crime: A prospective study. Journal of Research in Crime and Delinquency, 40, 71-94.
67. Widom, C.S. & Maxfield, M.G. (2001). An update on the "cycle of violence." Washington, DC: U.S. Department of Justice. National Institute of Justice.
68. Cyr, M., McDu_, P., & Wright, J. (2006). Prevalence and predictions of dating violence among adolescent female victims of child sexual abuse. Journal of Interpersonal Violence, 21(8), 1000-1017.
69. Yates, T. M. (2004). The developmental psychopathology of self-injurious behavior: Compensatory regulation in posttraumatic adaptation. Clinical Psychology Review, 24(1), 35-74.
70. Douglas, E., & Finkelhor, D. (2005). Childhood Sexual Abuse Fact Sheet. Crimes Against Children Center, University of New Hampshire. http://www.unh.edu/ccrc/factsheet/pdf/CSA-FS20.pdf
71. Carter, C. A., Bottoms, B. L., & Levine, M. (1996). Linguistic and socioemotional influences on the accuracy of children's reports. Law and Human Behavior, 20(3), 335-358.
72. Herrenkohl, E. C., Herrenkohl, R. C., Egolf, B. P., & Russo, M. J. (1998). The relationship between early maltreatment and teenage parenthood. Journal of Adolescence, 21, 291-303.
73. Raj, A., Silverman, J. G., & Amaro, H. (2000). The relationship between sexual abuse and sexual risk among high school students: Findings from the 1997 Massachusetts Youth Risk Behavior Survey. Maternal & Child Health Journal, 4(2), 125134.
74. Simpson, T.L. & Miller, W.R. (2002). Concomitance between childhood sexual and physical abuse and substance use problems: A review. Clinical Psychology Review, 22, 27-77.

75. Rohde, P., Ichikawa, L., Simon, G. E., Ludman, E. J., Linde, J. A. Jeffery, R. W., & Operskalski, B. H. (2008). Associations of child sexual and physical abuse with obesity and depression in middle-aged women. Child Abuse & Neglect, 32, 878– 887.
76. Dube, S. A., Anda, R. F., Whitfield, C. L., Brown, D. W., Felitti, D. J., Dong, M., & Giles, W. (2005). Long-term consequences of childhood sexual abuse by gender of the victim. American Journal of Preventive Medicine, 28, 430 – 437.
77. Waldrop, A. E. Hanson, R. F., Resnick, H. S., Kilpatrick, D. G., Naugle, A. E., & Saunders, B. E. (2007). Risk factors for suicidal behavior among a national sample of adolescents: Implications for prevention. Journal of Traumatic Stress, 20, 869 – 879.
78. Day, A., Thurlow, K., & Woolliscroft, J. (2003). Working with childhood sexual abuse: A survey of mental health professionals.Child Abuse & Neglect, 27, 191-198.
79. Kendler, K., Bulik, C., Silberg, J., Hettema, J., Myers, J., & Prescott, C. (2000). Childhood sexual abuse and adult psychiatric and substance use disorders in women: An epidemiological and Cotwin Control Analysis. Archives of General Psychiatry, 57, 953-959.
80. Voeltanz, N., Wilsnack, S., Harris, R., Wilsnack, R., Wonderlich, S., Kristjanson, A. (1999). Prevalence and risk for childhood sexual abuse in women : National survey findings. Child Abuse and Neglect, 23, 579-592.
81. Walrath, C., Ybarra, M., Holden, W., Liao, Q., Santiago, R., & Leaf, R. (2003). Children with reported histories of sexual abuse: Utilizing multiple perspectives to understand clinical and psychological profiles. Child Abuse & Neglect, 27, 509524.
82. Fuemmeler, B. F., Dedert, E., McClernon, F. J., & Beckham, J. C. (2009). Adverse childhood events are associated with obesity and disordered eating: Results from a U.S. population-based survey of young adults. Journal of Traumatic Stress, 22, 329 – 333.

83. Arnow, B. A. (2004). Relationships between childhood maltreatment, adult health and psychiatric outcomes, and medical utilization. Journal of Clinical Psychiatry, 65 [suppl 12], 10 – 15.
84. Sachs-Ericsson, N., Blazer, D., Plant, E. A., & Arnow, B. (2005). Childhood sexual and physical abuse and 1-year prevalence of medical problems in the National Comorbidity Survey. Health Psychology, 24, 32 – 40.
85. Golding, J. M., Cooper, M. L., & George, L. K. (1997). Sexual assault history and health perceptions: Seven general population studies. Health Psychology, 16, 417 – 425.
86. Newman, M. G., Clayton, L., Zuellig, A., Cashman, L., Arnow, B., Dea, R., & Taylor, C. B. (2000). The relationship of childhood sexual abuse and depression with somatic symptoms and medical utilization. Psychological Medicine, 30, 1063 – 1077.
87. Walker, E. A., Keegan, D., Gardner, G., Sullivan, M., Bernstein, D. & Katon, W. J. (1997). Psychosocial factors in fibromyalgia compared with rheumatoid arthritis: II. Sexual, physical, and emotional abuse and neglect. Psychosomatic Medicine, 59, 572 – 577.
88. Finkelhor, D., & Ormrod, R. (2001). Child Abuse Reported to the Police. Juvenile Justice Bulletin, (No. NCJ 187238). Washington, DC: United States Department of Justice, Office of Juvenile Justice and Delinquency Prevention.
89. Golding, J. M. (1996). Sexual assault history and women's reproductive and sexual health.Psychology of Women Quarterly, 20, 101 – 121.
90. Wilson, H. & Widom, C.S. (2009). An examination of risky sexual behavior and HIV among victims of child abuse and neglect: A thirty-year follow-up. Health Psychology, 27, 149-158
91. Dekker, A. et. al. (1990). The incidence of sexual abuse in HIV infected adolescents and young adults. Journal of Adolescent Health Care. vol. 11, no. 3.
92. Fang, X., Brown, D., Florence, C., Mercy, J. (2012) The economic burden of child maltreatment in the United States and implications for prevention. Child Abuse & Neglect, 36:2,156–165

www.ingramcontent.com/pod-product-compliance
Lightning Source LLC
Chambersburg PA
CBHW050828160426
43192CB00010B/1935